Use of English

Ten more practice tests for the
Cambridge C1 Advanced

Billie Jago

With an introduction by Michael Macdonald

PROSPERITY EDUCATION

PROSPERITY EDUCATION

www.prosperityeducation.net

Registered offices: Sherlock Close, Cambridge
CB3 0HP, United Kingdom

© Prosperity Education Ltd. 2020

First published March 2020
Revised edition July 2020

ISBN: 978-1-9161297-7-1

Manufactured on demand by Kindle Direct Publishing.

'Use of English', Cambridge C1 Advanced' and 'CAE' are brands
belonging to The Chancellor, Masters and Scholars of the
University of Cambridge and are not associated with
Prosperity Education or its products.

The moral rights of the author have been asserted.

For further information and resources, visit:
www.prosperityeducation.net

To infinity and beyond.

Contents

Introduction

Welcome to this second edition of sample tests for the Cambridge C1 Advanced, Use of English (Parts 1–4).

The pass threshold of the Cambridge C1 Advanced (CAE) examination is 60% and so, in order to allow ample time for the reading parts (Parts 5–8) of Paper 1, it is advisable that candidates complete The Use of English section (Parts 1–4) as quickly as possible while maintaining accuracy. For instance, completing each part in fewer than five minutes will allow 55 minutes in which to complete the reading parts.

This resource comprises ten whole Use of English tests, answer keys, write-in answer sheets and a marking scheme, allowing you to score each test out of 36 marks.

Author Billie Jago is a Cambridge-based ELT writer, teacher and teacher trainer, and has written ELT print and digital materials for Pearson Education, National Geographic, and educational organisations Education First and Wall Street English.

The content has been written to closely replicate the Cambridge exam experience, and has undergone comprehensive expert and peer review. You or your students, if you are a teacher, will hopefully enjoy the wide range of essay topics and benefit from the repetitive practice, something that is key to preparing for this part of the C1 Advanced (CAE) examination.

For me, having prepared many students for this and other Cambridge exams, pre- and post-2015, when the specification changed, this is clearly the section that poses the biggest challenge. Without there being much support available by way of quality practice material, students struggle to gain the necessary levels of confidence in the Use of English section prior to sitting the exam. Therefore, in my classes, after studying and working through the core knowledge required, we drill, drill and drill exercises in preparation for the exams.

I hope that you will find this resource a useful study aid, and I wish you all the best in preparing for the exam.

Michael Macdonald
Madrid, 2020

About the C1 Advanced exam

The Use of English section of the C1 Advanced (CAE) exam is broken down into four parts:

Part 1. Multiple choice cloze	
What is being tested?	This part of the exam mostly tests vocabulary, idioms, collocations, shades of meaning, phrasal verbs, complementation, semantic precision and fixed phrases.
How does it work?	It contains a test with eight gaps, each gap prompting multiple-choice questions. Each question has four possible answers, only one of which is correct.
How is it marked?	One mark is awarded for each correct answer.

Part 2. Open cloze	
What is being tested?	This part of the exam has a lexico-grammatical focus, testing candidates' awareness and control of grammar, fixed phrasing, collocation, semantic precision and, to an extent, vocabulary (the particles/prepositions for phrasal verbs).
How does it work?	It contains a text with eight gaps, each gap representing a missing word. No hints are given: candidates must think of the correct word for each gap.
How is it marked?	One mark is awarded for each correct answer.

Part 3. Word formation	
What is being tested?	This part of the exam focuses on affixation, internal changes and compounding in word formation, and vocabulary.
How does it work?	It contains a text with eight gaps, each gap representing a missing word. Beside each gap is a 'prompt' word that must be altered in some way to complete the sentence correctly.
How is it marked?	One mark is awarded for each correct answer.

Part 4. Key word transformations	
What is being tested?	This part of the exam has a lexico-grammatical focus, testing lexis, grammar and vocabulary.
How does it work?	It contains six sentences, each followed by a 'key' word and an alternative sentence conveying the same meaning as the first but with a gap in the middle. Candidates are to use the keyword provided to complete the second sentence so that it has a similar meaning to the first sentence. Candidates cannot change the keyword provided.
How is it marked?	Each correct answer is broken down into two marks.

PROSPERITY EDUCATION
www.prosperityeducation.net

Cambridge
C1 Advanced
Use of English

Test 1

For questions 1–8, read the text below and decide which answer best fits each gap. In the separate answer sheet, mark the appropriate answer (A, B, C or D).

The world's happiest country

For the past three years, Norway has been **(1)**_____ number one in the UN's World Happiness Report – the list of the happiest countries in the world.

In 2017, Norway **(2)**_____ Denmark because of its sense of community, education system, work–life balance and the personal freedoms its citizens enjoy. **(3)**_____ some parts of the country not getting any sunlight for a large part of the year, the Norwegians suggest that their 'hygge' lifestyle – a feeling of contentment and well-being through the simple things in life – is one of the reasons for their success. Their generous parental leave and flexibility at work gives them time to **(4)**_____ their personal interests, and the country is also **(5)**_____ considered one of the best in the world in which to be a mother and a working woman. There is **(6)**_____ no gender pay gap, and there are free childcare places for all children over the age of one.

So, what other countries made the Top 10? Denmark, Norway and Finland were next, followed by The Netherlands and Switzerland. Further **(7)**_____, New Zealand, Canada and Australia took spots 8, 9 and 10. In fact, each of these countries has something in common, and analysts believe this might have something to do with the level of happiness displayed among their citizens. Each country has a relatively small population compared to its size, and lots of tranquil, almost untouched outdoor spaces that provide enough room for people to **(8)**_____ and find their own corner of paradise.

1	A	ranked	B	numbered	C	placed	D	put
2	A	kicked out	B	knocked	C	displaced	D	removed
3	A	Although	B	However	C	But	D	Despite
4	A	pursue	B	chase	C	undertake	D	follow
5	A	highly	B	widely	C	slightly	D	nearly
6	A	only	B	almost	C	still	D	yet
7	A	ahead	B	distance	C	ashore	D	afield
8	A	stock up	B	make room	C	spread out	D	lay out

For questions 9–16, read the text below and decide which word best fits each gap. Use only one word for each gap. In the separate answer sheet, write your answers in capital letters, using one box per letter.

Las Fallas

Las Fallas is the one of the biggest street festivals in Europe and is held annually in Valencia, Spain's third-largest city.

The festivities occur throughout the month of March and include daily firework displays known **(9)**_____ *La Mascleta*, and traditional Valencian costumes **(10)**_____ display, worn by local *falleras* (females) and *falleros* (males). One of the best things about the festival is the unveiling of the cartoon-like installations, **(11)**_____ every *barrio*, or area, has designed and made. Some depict satirical scenes, political figures or even romantic stories. On March 19th each year, **(12)**_____ installation is set on fire, except one – the 14-metre- high Virgin Mary statue in one of Valencia's main squares. Here, flowers are offered to her **(13)**_____ what is called *La Ofrenda*. This flowery figure remains in one piece for two–three weeks after Las Fallas ends.

The origins of the festival are uncertain, but it's thought to **(14)**_____ come from the ancient tradition of starting fires to celebrate the change of seasons. The first written record to mention Fallas is from the second half of the 18th century, **(15)**_____ the Valencian government made laws governing where fires could be set.

By the morning after *La Crema*, the final night of the Las Fallas celebration, everything will have **(16)**_____ meticulously cleaned up, leaving no trace of the festival ever happening … until the next year.

For questions 17–24, use the stem word on the right to form the correct word that fills each gap. In the separate answer sheet, write your answers in capital letters, using one box per letter.

Mudlarking

An unusual hobby for some, mudlarking – looking for rare objects next to a tidal river – is becoming (17)_____ popular. The number of people requesting (18)_____ from the Port Authority of London to do this reached new highs last year. A recent survey has shown that (19)_____ are seeing their hobby as a way to (20)_____ and recycle old treasures, but, recently, many mudlarkers have seen a (21)_____ number of plastic bottles, wet wipes, and plastic bags on the river banks; the (22)_____ signature of today's throwaway society.

INCREASE
PERMIT

ENTHUSE
USE

WORRY

MISTAKE

When the tide goes out, the top layer of shingle appears through a patch of mud. Often, a variety of washed-up artefacts are revealed. Some may be of historical (23)_____, but most are simply bits of unused, old junk. However, some of the more valuable items recently discovered on the banks of the River Thames include Victorian china, 16th-century clay pipe bowls, Medieval pots and Roman roof tiles. From these items, mudlarkers believe they can find out more about their city and raise (24)_____ of the issues that many of our rivers are facing – waste and plastic pollution.

SIGNIFY

AWARE

For questions 25–30, complete the second sentence, using the word given, so that it has a similar meaning to the first sentence. Do not change the word provided and use between three and six words in total. In the separate answer sheet, write your answers in capital letters, using one box per letter.

25   The letter said we didn't have to reply.

   OBLIGATION

   We were _____ reply to the letter.

26   My house in London is much smaller than my house in Paris.

   NEARLY

   My house in London is _____ my house in Paris.

27   They'll blame the failure of the experiment on the lack of research.

   DOWN

   The failure of the experiment _____ the lack of research.

28   If I hadn't had your help, I would've failed my driving test.

   FOR

   Had it _____, I would've failed my driving test.

29   It's impossible you saw Max last night, because he was with me!

   HAVE

   You _____ last night, because he was with me!

30   I tried so hard to stop him interfering in our lives, but I couldn't.

   PREVENT

   I couldn't _____ in our lives.

Answer sheet: Cambridge C1 Advanced
Use of English

Test No. ☐

Mark out of 36 ☐

Name _____ **Date** _____

Part 1: Multiple choice

8 marks

Mark the appropriate answer (A, B, C or D).

0	A	B	C	D
	—	▬	—	—

1	A	B	C	D		5	A	B	C	D
	—	—	—	—			—	—	—	—

2	A	B	C	D		6	A	B	C	D
	—	—	—	—			—	—	—	—

3	A	B	C	D		7	A	B	C	D
	—	—	—	—			—	—	—	—

4	A	B	C	D		8	A	B	C	D
	—	—	—	—			—	—	—	—

Part 2: Open cloze

8 marks

Write your answers in capital letters, using one box per letter.

0	B	E	C	A	U	S	E				

9											
10											
11											
12											
13											
14											
15											
16											

Part 3: Word formation   8 marks

Write your answers in capital letters, using one box per letter.

17										

18										

19										

20										

21										

22										

23										

24										

Part 4: Key word transformation   12 marks

Write your answers in capital letters, using one box per letter.

25																	

26																	

27																	

28																	

29																	

30																	

Cambridge C1 Advanced Use of English

Test 2

For questions 1–8, read the text below and decide which answer best fits each gap. In the separate answer sheet, mark the appropriate answer (A, B, C or D).

The Japanese tea ceremony

Also known as *The Way of Tea*, the Japanese tea ceremony is the cultural **(1)**_____ of preparing and serving green tea.

One of its main purposes is for guests to enjoy the **(2)**_____ of their host in an **(3)**_____ far from the everyday worries and stresses of life. It begins with a silent bow, then a 'purification' in a stone basin – washing hands and rinsing the mouth with water. After this, guests remove their footwear before entering the tearoom. The ceremony takes place in a traditional Tatami room with mat-covered floors and cushions to kneel on.

The host typically prepares the tea in front of the guests. They use **(4)**_____ such as a tea whisk, a tea container, a scoop, a bowl and a plate for sweets eaten before the tea. Everything used is ritually **(5)**_____, before the guest of **(6)**_____ is given the first sip. They then wipe the rim of the bowl and pass it to the next guest, who rotates it before drinking, representing respect and harmony.

Tea was once only drunk in Japan for medicinal purposes, but started to **(7)**_____ popularity in the 13th century. People began holding tea-drinking parties, where participants would bring their best tea bowls and boast about their knowledge of the drink. During this period, the **(8)**_____ Sen no Rikyu, also known as the father of *The Way of Tea*, designed a more simplistic way of enjoying the beverage. Nowadays, most schools that train masters of the tea ceremony use his spiritual teachings.

1	A	procedure	B	policy	C	service	D	ritual
2	A	welcome	B	hospitality	C	reception	D	work
3	A	atmosphere	B	aura	C	instance	D	element
4	A	contraptions	B	equipment	C	machines	D	gadgets
5	A	cleansed	B	washed up	C	decontaminated	D	fumigated
6	A	status	B	important	C	prestige	D	honour
7	A	gain	B	win	C	earn	D	get
8	A	valued	B	revered	C	complimented	D	approved

For questions 9–16, read the text below and decide which word best fits each gap. Use only one word for each gap. In the separate answer sheet, write your answers in capital letters, using one box per letter.

The throwaway society

We've all become used to today's 'throwaway society', **(9)**_____ that we all buy things and don't think twice about throwing them away as soon as they break or suffer a slight blemish **(10)**_____ scratch. However, some people have begun to upcycle their unloved goods, transforming them from useless waste into products of better quality and higher environmental value.

Initially a concept taken from a German book by Gunter Pauli, their goal is to prevent wasting potentially useful materials **(11)**_____ making use of existing ones. By doing **(12)**_____ we can reduce the consumption of new raw materials in the creation of products. This can lead to **(13)**_____ pollution, fewer greenhouse gas emissions and a general reduction in energy usage.

There are many ways to upcycle and **(14)**_____ of the more alternative methods include using a barrel as a coffee table, books as knife blocks, suitcases for shelving, and car parts or bathtubs as household furniture. People have even started using old boots as plant pots.

The industry-wide figures are unknown, but there has been significant growth in the **(15)**_____ of people selling upcycled products on handmade sites **(16)**_____ as Etsy. For example, in the period 2011–2014, upcycling saw an 879% growth in online search numbers. Analysts believe this number will grow exponentially over the coming years, as people begin to do more to tackle the threats facing our planet.

For questions 17–24, use the stem word on the right to form the correct word that fills each gap. In the separate answer sheet, write your answers in capital letters, using one box per letter.

On the brink of extinction

An extremely important – yet underappreciated – insect is in danger of becoming extinct. If this were to happen, it would destroy the delicate balance of the Earth's ecosystem and affect global food supplies.

We know that honeybees, bumble bees and solitary bees (17)_____ food crops. This process involves **POLLEN** insects moving pollen from one plant to another, (18)_____ the plants so they can produce vital **FERTILISE** food resources such as fruit, vegetables and seeds. By losing these (19)_____ species, pollination **THREAT** would be (20)_____ impacted, potentially wiping **GREAT** out entire plant species on which we rely for food.

One cause of the issue is the use of insecticides in fields, which can have devastating (21)_____ for the **IMPLY** countryside, and therefore a bee's health. Another contributor is 'urban beekeeping', which reduces the wild bee (22)_____. Global warming is also believed **POPULATE** to be a major factor in the decline of wild-bee numbers, as some bees can only survive within a narrow range of (23)_____. As habitats get warmer, the areas in **TEMPERATE** which bees can live become more limited.

As the bee population slowly declines, other insects begin to take their place, so it becomes (24)_____ that we will lose the crops we rely so **LIKE** heavily upon anytime soon. However, the loss of bees would certainly threaten our ecological stability.

For questions 25–30, complete the second sentence, using the word given, so that it has a similar meaning to the first sentence. Do not change the word provided and use between three and six words in total. In the separate answer sheet, write your answers in capital letters, using one box per letter.

25 I feel sometimes as if my boss doesn't appreciate me.

GRANTED

I feel as if my boss _____ sometimes.

26 James wondered how likely it was that the match would go ahead today.

CHANCES

James wondered what _____ the match going ahead today.

27 Her performance in the show today was nowhere near as good as last week's performance.

CONSIDERABLY

Her performance last week _____ than today.

28 "A sensible person wouldn't act that way", said Jake.

HOW

Jake said that was _____ would react.

29 'Daniela completed the task efficiently', the manager said.

CARRIED

The manager said Daniela _____ efficiently.

30 Without Selina's support, I don't think I'd have been able to face today.

BEEN

If _____ Selina's support, I don't think I would've been able to face today.

Answer sheet: Cambridge C1 Advanced
Use of English

Test No. ☐

Mark out of 36 ☐

Name _____   **Date** _____

Part 1: Multiple choice   8 marks

Mark the appropriate answer (A, B, C or D).

0	A	**B**	C	D

1	A	B	C	D		5	A	B	C	D

2	A	B	C	D		6	A	B	C	D

3	A	B	C	D		7	A	B	C	D

4	A	B	C	D		8	A	B	C	D

Part 2: Open cloze   8 marks

Write your answers in capital letters, using one box per letter.

0	B	E	C	A	U	S	E				

9											
10											
11											
12											
13											
14											
15											
16											

Part 3: Word formation

8 marks

Write your answers in capital letters, using one box per letter.

17										

18										

19										

20										

21										

22										

23										

24										

Part 4: Key word transformation

12 marks

Write your answers in capital letters, using one box per letter.

25																

26																

27																

28																

29																

30																

Cambridge C1 Advanced Use of English

Test 3

For questions 1–8, read the text below and decide which answer best fits each gap. In the separate answer sheet, mark the appropriate answer (A, B, C or D).

Monument Valley

Located on the Utah-Arizona **(1)**_____ in the US, Monument Valley sits **(2)**_____ the Navajo Tribal Park and is now one of the most photographed places on Earth.

Thanks to it being **(3)**_____ featured in a number of famous films and TV shows such as *Forrest Gump*, *Mission Impossible II* and the HBO series *Westworld*, it has recently begun to gain popularity among visitors to the area.

It is part of the Navajo Nation, the largest Native American territory in the United States, and, **(4)**_____ the area is protected as a national park would be, the Navajo Park is owned by the locals so therefore has its own set of rules. For example, the Park has its own time zone and follows its own governance, and the area has a microclimate – the temperature can sometimes **(5)**_____ below zero degrees at night.

So, what exactly is Monument Valley, and how was it formed?

Before human **(6)**_____, the area was a flat plain. Over millions of years, **(7)**_____ of the Rocky Mountains deposited layer upon layer of sediment, which, mixed with magma rising from the Earth's crust, allowed for the plateau to form. Natural forces have spent years chipping **(8)**_____ at the plateau, which has formed the stunning natural wonders seen in Monument Valley today.

1	**A**	border	**B** frontier	**C** division	**D** territory
2	**A**	into	**B** within	**C** on	**D** at
3	**A**	rigorously	**B** thoroughly	**C** steadily	**D** heavily
4	**A**	however	**B** whereas	**C** although	**D** but
5	**A**	lower	**B** dip	**C** submerge	**D** collapse
6	**A**	reality	**B** survival	**C** existence	**D** actuality
7	**A**	lacerations	**B** decay	**C** decomposition	**D** erosion
8	**A**	around	**B** by	**C** away	**D** over

For questions 9–16, read the text below and decide which word best fits each gap. Use only one word for each gap. In the separate answer sheet, write your answers in capital letters, using one box per letter.

The Great Wall of China

The Great Wall of China is widely thought to date **(9)**_____ 2000 years, to just after 221 BC when China was unified. It was commissioned by the First Emperor to protect his subjects from the Xiongnu, a group of nomads that inhabited the eastern Eurasian Steppe, which stretches from modern-day Bulgaria to Mongolia.

Often labelled as **(10)**_____ of the greatest wonders of the world, over ten million people visit the Wall each year. However, many who come to visit are surprised to find that it is **(11)**_____ one continuous stretch of wall. It is a series of fortifications that were built during different dynasties over thousands of years. **(12)**_____ the 21,196 kilometres of wall, nearly half were constructed by the Ming Dynasty, which ruled from 1368–1644. Today, these are the most visited and best-preserved sections of the Wall, totalling 6,259 kilometres in length.

There are many myths surrounding the Wall – one being that it can be seen from outer Space. **(13)**_____, many astronauts have disproved this claim, stating that 'the materials used to build the wall are similar in colour and texture to the materials of the surrounding land'. **(14)**_____ legend proposes that many builders of the Wall are actually buried inside it, but, **(15)**_____ date, no bone fragments have been discovered. **(16)**_____ this fact, the Wall still carries the nickname of 'the longest cemetery on Earth', as over a million labourers are estimated to have died during its construction.

For questions 17–24, use the stem word on the right to form the correct word that fills each gap. In the separate answer sheet, write your answers in capital letters, using one box per letter.

Bossaball

A unique blend of sport, music and gymnastics, Bossaball is a relatively new sport taking Europe by storm.

Invented by Filip Eyckmans from Belgium in 2004, it has seen its **(17)**_____ grow in recent times, particularly in Spain and the Netherlands. In fact, the Netherlands has even launched its own major Bossaball league.
POPULAR

Similar to volleyball, the **(18)**_____ of the game is to ground the ball on the opponent's side of the court, earning points based on where the ball lands. The game is held on a court consisting of **(19)**_____ panels, trampolines and a net, with only one player on the court at a time. The 'samba referee', who **(20)**_____ the game, not only makes the decisions, but also provides musical **(21)**_____ to the action, using a whistle, microphone, percussion instruments and a DJ set. The name Bossaball is therefore fitting, since music is a major component of how the game is played. Players are free to dive, kick, flip and dance their way to passing the ball over the net in any which way they can, and the music creates a buzz that spectators **(22)**_____ partake in.
OBJECT

INFLATE

SEE
ACCOMPANY

ENTHUSE

So, what's next for the sport? With a World Cup already taking place, Bossaball is aiming to make its way to the Olympics. It has recently been hailed as one of the most **(23)**_____ acrobatic and energetic games of our time, providing a low-impact workout, muscle-toning and improving one's **(24)**_____.
Why not give it a try?
UNIQUE

COORDINATE

For questions 25–30, complete the second sentence, using the word given, so that it has a similar meaning to the first sentence. Do not change the word provided and use between three and six words in total. In the separate answer sheet, write your answers in capital letters, using one box per letter.

25   The local council is demolishing the block of old flats opposite the park.

      PULLED

      The old block of flats opposite the park _____ council.

26   Antonio didn't feel like going into work today.

      MOOD

      Antonio _____ going to work today.

27   I wish I was taller because then I'd be a professional basketball player.

      ONLY

      _____ taller, I'd be a professional basketball player.

28   I get on really well with my brother's new wife.

      TERMS

      I'm _____ my brother's new wife.

29   If James didn't think of a solution to the problem, he'd be fired.

      COME

      James had to _____ to the problem or he'd be fired.

30   Even though I'd been studying more than ever, my grades had only got a little bit better this term.

      SLIGHTLY

      My grades _____ this term than they were before, even though I'd been studying hard.

Answer sheet: Cambridge C1 Advanced
Use of English

Test No. ☐

Mark out of 36 ☐

Name _____   **Date** _____

Part 1: Multiple choice   8 marks

Mark the appropriate answer (A, B, C or D).

0	A	**B**	C	D	

1	A	B	C	D			5	A	B	C	D
2	A	B	C	D			6	A	B	C	D
3	A	B	C	D			7	A	B	C	D
4	A	B	C	D			8	A	B	C	D

Part 2: Open cloze   8 marks

Write your answers in capital letters, using one box per letter.

0	B	E	C	A	U	S	E				

9										
10										
11										
12										
13										
14										
15										
16										

Part 3: Word formation   8 marks

Write your answers in capital letters, using one box per letter.

17											
18											
19											
20											
21											
22											
23											
24											

Part 4: Key word transformation   12 marks

Write your answers in capital letters, using one box per letter.

25																
26																
27																
28																
29																
30																

Cambridge
C1 Advanced
Use of English

Test 4

For questions 1–8, read the text below and decide which answer best fits each gap. In the separate answer sheet, mark the appropriate answer (A, B, C or D).

Spotify

Spotify is a music-streaming platform that was designed in an attempt to create a service to tackle piracy in the music industry. Before it came along, controversial file-sharing sites like LimeWire and Napster were used to illegally download and share songs online. Spotify founders Daniel Ek and Martin Lorentzon wanted to solve this problem.

(1)_____ in 2006 in Sweden, the Spotify app began to offer a free service in 2008, **(2)**_____ played advertisements and jingles between songs. The developers soon added a £10-a-month subscription service, which allowed users to listen ad-free.

Spotify's rise to the top has fought off **(3)**_____ competition from the likes of Apple Music, which had secured exclusive deals with many major artists **(4)**_____ as Taylor Swift and Drake. Stars began publicly speaking out **(5)**_____ Spotify for paying minimal royalties to artists for streaming their songs, so the developers started to add rising stars and independent artists to their music library in response.

Spotify is now estimated to be **(6)**_____ as much as $23.4 billion, but it has **(7)**_____ to make a profit. This is due to courts, particularly those in the US, forcing streaming services to pay more to the labels for the music they play. However, with over 170 million active users, Spotify's founders have **(8)**_____ the way people listen to the songs they love.

1	A	Grown	B	Developed	C	Made	D	Evolved
2	A	which	B	what	C	when	D	whose
3	A	stiff	B	tricky	C	rough	D	hard
4	A	so	B	like	C	such	D	long
5	A	to	B	against	C	from	D	for
6	A	cost	B	priced	C	valued	D	worth
7	A	since	B	already	C	yet	D	just
8	A	transformed	B	mutated	C	preserved	D	reshuffled

For questions 9–16, read the text below and decide which word best fits each gap. Use only one word for each gap. In the separate answer sheet, write your answers in capital letters, using one box per letter.

The National English Proficiency Test

A new English test, the National English Proficiency Test, also to be known as NATS, is **(9)**_____ launched in China next year. The test, **(10)**_____ will be rolled out in Summer 2020, aims to unify the varying standards and targets of English language testing across the country.

In 2014, China's State Council set out a reform for a 'standardised, functional and modern' new approach to learning English. Much research has **(11)**_____ carried out across various stages of education many Chinese provinces **(12)**_____ then. The Council found that a range of tests were being used with a mix of levels – proving unsuccessful in many cases – and there was therefore **(13)**_____ real standardised way of testing.

By unifying the standards, the National English Proficiency Test has been designed to assess candidates' practical language skills, cross-cultural awareness and communication skills, as well **(14)**_____ their ability across the four main areas – listening, speaking, reading and writing. Albert Cummings, chair of the TOEFL Committee of Examiners, hopes that the new test **(15)**_____ inspire a more authentic way of learning a language – something that will be necessary for many future students. The Ministry of Education in China says the country has **(16)**_____ a breakthrough in developing the first comprehensive-scale system for teaching in the country.

For questions 17–24, use the stem word on the right to form the correct word that fills each gap. In the separate answer sheet, write your answers in capital letters, using one box per letter.

Geocaching

More and more people are taking up the hobby of 'geocaching' – an exciting new outdoor activity for the digital **(17)**_____.   **GENERATE**

Geocaches, or caches, are small, hidden underwater treasure boxes that are **(18)**_____ out by   **SEEK** geocachers using individual GPS devices. These devices use compass coordinates downloaded from the Geocaching app to help you locate the many boxes planted around your local area. Inside each box, once discovered, you'll find a reward, or prize. Often, these are 'swap' items, so, if you take something, you'll need to bring another trinket to **(19)**_____ it with. So why   **PLACE** has this activity recently gained such a large **(20)**_____?   **FOLLOW**

In 2000, The US government discontinued **(21)**_____ available GPS signals. This meant that   **PUBLIC** the GPS could insert random signals that made **(22)**_____ determining your position impossible.   **ACCURATE** The purpose was to give the US military a strategic advantage using GPS hardware. However, they soon developed a more advanced technology that meant commercial GPS receivers could determine one's position within a range of 6–20 feet. Soon after, GPS-receiver enthusiast Dave Ulmer decided to hide a **(23)**_____ in a remote Oregon location, and post   **CONTAIN** its coordinates online. It took only three days for two individuals to find his geocache, and the hobby was born.

Following various suggested names for the new activity, the title 'geocaching' gained wide **(24)**_____ after   **ACCEPT** a hobbyist put the suggestion forward. The name consists of *geo*, meaning Earth, and *cache*, meaning a temporary storage location.

For questions 25–30, complete the second sentence, using the word given, so that it has a similar meaning to the first sentence. Do not change the word provided and use between three and six words in total. In the separate answer sheet, write your answers in capital letters, using one box per letter.

25   Every time the publisher talks about my book launch, I get more nervous.

   THE

   The more the publisher talks about my book launch,
   _____ become.

26   I'd never seen such a beautiful sunset in all my life.

   BEFORE

   Never _____ such a beautiful sunset.

27   I would prefer to go to Valencia than Barcelona if I had the option.

   RATHER

   Given the choice, _____ Valencia than Barcelona.

28   I don't like Rebecca because she always thinks she's better than everyone else.

   LOOKS

   Rebecca always _____ people, so I don't like her.

29   'If I can do anything to help you during this difficult time, sir, please do not hesitate to ask.'

   ASSISTANCE

   'Please let me know If I can _____ during this difficult time, sir.'

30   I'd registered to start learning Russian at the local language school.

   SIGNED

   I'd _____ classes at the local language school.

Answer sheet: Cambridge C1 Advanced
Use of English

Test No. [ ]

Mark out of 36 [ ]

Name _____ **Date** _____

Part 1: Multiple choice   8 marks

Mark the appropriate answer (A, B, C or D).

| 0 | A | **B** | C | D |

1	A	B	C	D		5	A	B	C	D
2	A	B	C	D		6	A	B	C	D
3	A	B	C	D		7	A	B	C	D
4	A	B	C	D		8	A	B	C	D

Part 2: Open cloze   8 marks

Write your answers in capital letters, using one box per letter.

| 0 | B | E | C | A | U | S | E | | | | |

9

10

11

12

13

14

15

16

Part 3: W

Write yo

17

18

19

20

21

22

23

24

Part 4: Key word transformation   12 marks

Write your answers in capital letters, using one box per letter.

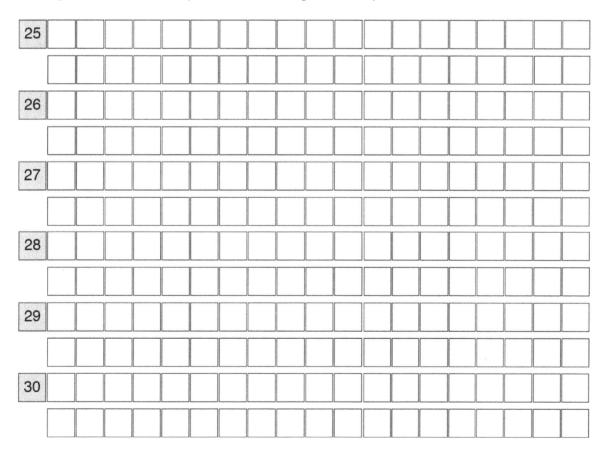

25

26

27

28

29

30

Cambridge C1 Advanced Use of English

Test 5

Queen

One of the world's best-selling music artists, Queen, has just announced a huge world tour in 2020, including ten consecutive performances in London.

Formed in 1970, the band originally consisted of guitarist Brian May and drummer Roger Taylor, and went **(1)**_____ the name of *Smile*. A fan of the band, Farrokh Bulsara, asked to join, changed the name to *Queen* and recruited a young bassist called John Deacon. Farrokh then took on a new **(2)**_____, Freddie Mercury, and began to take the band in a new direction. Their first ever **(3)**_____ as the now-famous foursome was outside a college building in London, in 1971.

Since then, they've sold over 300 million records, performed for the largest TV **(4)**_____ of all time (1.9 billion people), own a star on the Hollywood Walk of Fame and have the longest-running rock group fan club in the world. Since the tragic and untimely death of Freddie in 1991, the band have toured with a **(5)**_____ of frontmen to mixed reactions amongst fans, but, in 2011, Queen **(6)**_____ on *American Idol* **(7)**_____ Adam Lambert. Together, this line up has toured for more than 100 dates internationally in over 50 countries, and even did a ten-day residency in Las Vegas in 2018.

Queen's recent revival has **(8)**_____ been down to the success of the Queen biopic *Bohemian Rhapsody,* released in 2018, which received four Academy Awards, including Best Actor.

1	**A**	in	**B**	for	**C**	by	**D**	through
2	**A**	mask	**B**	pretence	**C**	disguise	**D**	persona
3	**A**	recital	**B**	gig	**C**	session	**D**	jam
4	**A**	onlookers	**B**	audience	**C**	spectators	**D**	observers
5	**A**	variety	**B**	assortment	**C**	array	**D**	miscellany
6	**A**	got	**B**	put	**C**	took	**D**	made
7	**A**	player	**B**	applicant	**C**	candidate	**D**	contestant
8	**A**	inexplicably	**B**	distinctly	**C**	undoubtedly	**D**	noticeably

For questions 9–16, read the text below and decide which word best fits each gap. Use only one word for each gap. In the separate answer sheet, write your answers in capital letters, using one box per letter.

The not-so-great British High Street

According to a recent study, the death of the British High Street may **(9)**_____ far sooner than people think. Growing up in 1950's Britain meant milkmen delivering to your door, greengrocers selling locally grown, fresh fruit and vegetables, and a local fishmonger doing the rounds in every street in the town. Fast forward to today, and a world of e-commerce and home delivery is said to be threatening the future of British shops and town centres.

The study has shown that, **(10)**_____ 2030, local town centres may be a distant memory due to e-commerce and home-delivery services.

Until recently, the High Streets of Britain **(11)**_____ changed very little since the rise of the supermarket in the 1960's. Nowadays, an average of five shops are closing every day, meaning more than 50,000 retail jobs **(12)**_____ lost in the last year alone. In 2019, more than 16,000 stores closed – the highest number of all time.

Another issue to consider is that, in many British towns **(13)**_____ is not uncommon to find four or five charity shops in one row, in **(14)**_____ used to be prime High Street locations. They sell second-hand, donated goods at a low price and donate their profits to charitable organisations. However, **(15)**_____ shops pay low commercial rental fees, which means that local councils are also losing out, but cannot find other retailers **(16)**_____ wish to open new units and pay a higher rent than their neighbours.

For questions 17–24, use the stem word on the right to form the correct word that fills each gap. In the separate answer sheet, write your answers in capital letters, using one box per letter.

A tale of time travel

Outlander is a (17)_____ television drama series that is a mix of both fact and fiction.   **HISTORY**

Based on a series of books with the same name by author Diana Gabaldon, it tells the story of a former British Army nurse, Claire Randall, who is (18)_____ swept   **MYSTERY**
back in time to the year 1743, during the rise of the Jacobites fighting against England. She is thrown into an
(19)_____ world where her life and freedom are   **KNOW**
(20)_____ threatened. She soon meets a   **CONSTANT**
complicated Highlander called James Fraser, whom Claire is forced to marry to save her life.

Fans of the original books, the first of which was published in 1991, waited a long time for the series to be premiered in 2014. Gabaldon has been writing the *Outlander* books ever since the first was published, with the
(21)_____ title, *Written in my own heart's blood,*   **LATE**
publishing in 2014. The series has received critical acclaim, with *The Huffington Post* calling the first episode
'a masterpiece of (22)_____ depth', and online   **IMPRESS**
entertainment website The A.V. Club calling it 'downright
(23)_____'.   **IMMERSE**

So, what's next for the show? It has been
(24)_____ for a sixth season, with the 13-episode   **NEW**
fifth season set to premiere in 2020. Both seasons will be an adaptation of the fifth and sixth books in the *Outlander* series and are eagerly anticipated by fans.

For questions 25–30, complete the second sentence, using the word given, so that it has a similar meaning to the first sentence. Do not change the word provided and use between three and six words in total. In the separate answer sheet, write your answers in capital letters, using one box per letter.

25   I had to invent a story to tell Maria why I wasn't at her party.

      UP

      Maria asked me why I didn't go to her party, so I had to
      _____ tell her.

26   I didn't hesitate to tell my manager the truth about what I'd done when she asked.

      HESITATION

      When my boss asked me what I'd done, I _____.

27   If you feel hot, drinking lots of water ought to cool you down.

      MAKE

      Drinking lots of water should _____ if you feel hot.

28   I don't have any money, so I can't get the tickets for the festival.

      WOULD

      If I had money, _____ for the festival.

29   Scientists claim they will have made a breakthrough by this time next year.

      CLAIMED

      It _____ will have made a breakthrough in a year's time.

30   Provided that the weather is good, we'll have a barbecue this weekend.

      LONG

      We'll have a barbecue this weekend, _____ is good.

Answer sheet: Cambridge C1 Advanced
Use of English

Test No. ☐

Mark out of 36 ☐

Name _____ **Date** _____

Part 1: Multiple choice   8 marks

Mark the appropriate answer (A, B, C or D).

| 0 | A | **B** | C | D |

1	A	B	C	D		5	A	B	C	D
2	A	B	C	D		6	A	B	C	D
3	A	B	C	D		7	A	B	C	D
4	A	B	C	D		8	A	B	C	D

Part 2: Open cloze   8 marks

Write your answers in capital letters, using one box per letter.

| 0 | B | E | C | A | U | S | E | | | | |

9										
10										
11										
12										
13										
14										
15										
16										

Part 3: Word formation
8 marks

Write your answers in capital letters, using one box per letter.

17
18
19
20
21
22
23
24

Part 4: Key word transformation
12 marks

Write your answers in capital letters, using one box per letter.

25
26
27
28
29
30

Cambridge C1 Advanced Use of English

Test 6

For questions 1–8, read the text below and decide which answer best fits each gap. In the separate answer sheet, mark the appropriate answer (A, B, C or D).

Argan oil

A natural oil extracted from the kernels of the argan tree, argan oil is beauty's latest new **(1)**_____.

(2)_____ in Morocco, argan oil is primarily marketed as a skin- and hair-care product. It is said to have anti-ageing **(3)**_____ but can also **(4)**_____ a range of skin conditions, including eczema, acne and psoriasis. Dermatologists have said that the oil contains acids that can **(5)**_____ your natural collagen production, leaving your skin looking firmer and plumper. In addition, argan oil is also being used in the culinary world as a replacement for common oils, and to add a **(6)**_____ of spice to a dish.

The production of argan oil has also boosted Morocco's economy, providing support to almost 2.2 million people in its main growing **(7)**_____ of Arganeraie. It offers employment to women in a relatively rural area, and is set to provide more, with the government now stepping up its efforts to increase the **(8)**_____ of its argan tree groves.

1	**A** trend	**B** mania	**C** style	**D** rage
2	**A** Starting	**B** Founding	**C** Originating	**D** Beginning
3	**A** properties	**B** duties	**C** functions	**D** factors
4	**A** assist	**B** repair	**C** help	**D** treat
5	**A** lift	**B** boost	**C** uplift	**D** amplify
6	**A** piece	**B** measurement	**C** hint	**D** slither
7	**A** local	**B** neighborhood	**C** nation	**D** region
8	**A** agriculture	**B** cultivation	**C** growing	**D** improvement

For questions 9–16, read the text below and decide which word best fits each gap. Use only one word for each gap. In the separate answer sheet, write your answers in capital letters, using one box per letter.

The flat cap

The flat cap has once again become popular, more than 600 years after **(9)**_____ was first required by law to be worn by men in England.

An Act of Parliament in Northern England imposed a rule in the 14th century that all males over the age of six **(10)**_____ wear woollen hats on Sundays and holidays in order to boost the wool trade. However, this order only applied to the **(11)**_____-called lower classes. If they failed to abide **(12)**_____ the rule, they would be fined and ordered to pay three farthings per day – around £0.003p **(13)**_____ today's money.

By the 1920's, the popularity of the flat cap **(14)**_____ spread throughout the various social classes, and began to become fashionable overseas, particularly in the United States of America. There, it could be seen on the head of almost every man from every economic background on every occasion. However, in the decade that followed, its popularity with the younger generation had worn **(15)**_____, and it quickly became a staple only for older men.

Recently, the cap has seen a resurgence, with the popular BBC TV show *Peaky Blinders* inspiring a new generation of flat cap wearers. In 2019, flat cap sales were at an **(16)**_____-time high, even beating those of Amazon's Alexa.

For questions 17–24, use the stem word on the right to form the correct word that fills each gap. In the separate answer sheet, write your answers in capital letters, using one box per letter.

Barack Obama

Barack Hussein Obama served as the 44th President of the United States from 2009–2017. A member of the Democratic Party, he became the first African-American President to serve in office.

Barack was born and raised in Hawaii by his parents Barack Obama Sr., and Ann Dunham. His father was of Luo **(17)**_____ and came from the Nyanza **ETHNIC** Province of Kenya, where he eventually gained a **(18)**_____ to pursue his dreams of going to **SCHOLAR** college in the US. It was there that he met Barack's mother.

Six months after their **(19)**_____ ceremony, **MARRY** Barack was born. Sadly, shortly after this, the couple's relationship began to break down, and they divorced two years later. After some time, Barack's mother remarried, and the family **(20)**_____ to Indonesia, where **LOCATE** Barack's stepfather was **(21)**_____ from. **ORIGIN**

Five years later, after several incidents and a growing concern for his safety, Barack was sent back to Hawaii to live with his maternal grandparents. There, he began to excel in school and graduated with academic honours in 1979. After obtaining two degrees – one in **(22)**_____ science and the second in law – he **POLITICS** began to work in the south side of Chicago, known for its poverty, as a community **(23)**_____ working with **ORGANISE** low-income residents. This saw him bringing together local people to take **(24)**_____ action and put pressure **COLLECT** on local officials to fix problems in their neighborhoods. Many say this is where Barack got his first taste of what it would mean to be a politician.

For questions 25–30, complete the second sentence, using the word given, so that it has a similar meaning to the first sentence. Do not change the word provided and use between three and six words in total. In the separate answer sheet, write your answers in capital letters, using one box per letter.

25 We should take advantage of the fact that we are in an all-inclusive hotel!

    MOST

    We should _____ in an all-inclusive hotel!

26 'The whole team is really disappointed in your performance today,' Coach Burton said to me.

    LET

    Coach Burton said my performance really _____ today.

27 Recently, the number of people who are earning above minimum wage has gone up.

    INCREASE

    There _____ the number of people who are earning higher than the minimum wage.

28 I wish I had gone to the gig, because I was so bored at home on my own!

    ONLY

    If _____ to the gig, I wouldn't have been bored at home on my own!

29 Pablo told me to call him if I ever needed anything.

    CALL

    'Do not _____ you need something,' said Pablo.

30 It was bad of you to stay out late without letting me know.

    OUGHT

    You _____ you were staying out late.

Answer sheet: Cambridge C1 Advanced
Use of English

Test No. ☐

Mark out of 36 ☐

Name _____ **Date** _____

Part 1: Multiple choice   8 marks

Mark the appropriate answer (A, B, C or D).

0	A	B	C	D	

1	A	B	C	D	

| 2 | A | B | C | D | |

| 3 | A | B | C | D | |

| 4 | A | B | C | D | |

5	A	B	C	D	

| 6 | A | B | C | D | |

| 7 | A | B | C | D | |

| 8 | A | B | C | D | |

Part 2: Open cloze   8 marks

Write your answers in capital letters, using one box per letter.

0	B	E	C	A	U	S	E				

9											
10											
11											
12											
13											
14											
15											
16											

Part 3: Word formation   8 marks

Write your answers in capital letters, using one box per letter.

17											

18											

19											

20											

21											

22											

23											

24											

Part 4: Key word transformation   12 marks

Write your answers in capital letters, using one box per letter.

25																

26																

27																

28																

29																

30																

Cambridge C1 Advanced Use of English

Test 7

For questions 1–8, read the text below and decide which answer best fits each gap. In the separate answer sheet, mark the appropriate answer (A, B, C or D).

The National Geographic Society

On January 27th, 1888, the National Geographic Society was **(1)**_____ in Washington D.C.. Its original aim was to increase geographical knowledge amongst ordinary **(2)**_____.

The Society was started by a group of 33 men who worked as, among other professions, geographers, teachers, explorers and lawyers. **(3)**_____, they shared a passion for the Earth and its science, and believed that people were also curious about the world they lived in.

Their first step was to **(4)**_____ a magazine in October of the same year, but, unfortunately, only around 1000 readers overall took an **(5)**_____ over the whole decade, up until 1900. A new editor joined in 1899 and, from there, by adding photographs of wildlife and nature, the annual circulation **(6)**_____ to two million. It was **(7)**_____ the first magazine to print natural-colour photos. The Society used the magazine revenues to **(8)**_____ research expeditions around the world, and today, the National Geographic Society is one of the world's largest non-profit institutions.

1	**A**	began	**B**	discovered	**C**	founded	**D**	started
2	**A**	society	**B**	people	**C**	residents	**D**	inhabitants
3	**A**	Collectively	**B**	Generally	**C**	Entirely	**D**	Wholly
4	**A**	publish	**B**	deliver	**C**	publicise	**D**	announce
5	**A**	intrigue	**B**	attention	**C**	interest	**D**	regard
6	**A**	ascended	**B**	rose	**C**	lifted	**D**	hiked
7	**A**	eventually	**B**	finally	**C**	inevitably	**D**	actually
8	**A**	fee	**B**	spend	**C**	pay	**D**	fund

For questions 9–16, read the text below and decide which word best fits each gap. Use only one word for each gap. In the separate answer sheet, write your answers in capital letters, using one box per letter.

Tap dancing

In the early 19th century, a new style of dance **(9)**_____ born in the United States and remains popular to this day.

Tap dancing emerged as an art form through the fusion of several traditional dance styles and songs from a variety of cultures – the Irish jig, English clog dances and African tribal dances. It has **(10)**_____ suggested that 'tap', as it is known, was nurtured in certain environments of New York City, **(11)**_____ a mix of ethnic groups all lived together under crowded conditions in one neighborhood. One of the earliest known tap dancers was a performer called Master Juba, **(12)**_____ style of dancing involved wearing hard-soled shoes, or nailed boots. It was not **(13)**_____ the 20th century that metal taps – introduced by Broadway dancers – appeared on the soles of dancers' shoes.

Tap, unlike other forms of dancing, relies on its technique to be transmitted not only visually but aurally, and often with audience participation in the beat or a rhythmic exchange between dancers. Tap requires **(14)**_____ performers to use **(15)**_____ in-built rhythm to create a synergy between duos or groups of dancers, and facial expressions to show the emotion of the story that the performers' feet are telling.

Tap dancing saw a decline in popularity in the 1950's due to an increased interest **(16)**_____ ballet and more classical styles of dance, but it was revived some years later in variety shows that began to take place in Las Vegas' many theatres.

For questions 17–24, use the stem word on the right to form the correct word that fills each gap. In the separate answer sheet, write your answers in capital letters, using one box per letter.

Accents and dialects in the UK

UK bank HSBC has released the results of a study claiming that, over the next 50 years, language and speech in the UK as we currently know it will **(17)**_____ change.   **SIGNIFY**

The introduction of technology has already **(18)**_____ the way in which we speak, and the   **SHORT** study suggests that regional accents could die out **(19)**_____. It also proposes that future   **ENTIRE** **(20)**_____ with computers and technology will be   **INTERACT** executed through voice control, rather than keyboards.

Dominic Watt, a sociolinguistics expert at the University of York, was commissioned by HSBC to conduct the survey and produce a report of his **(21)**_____. He   **FIND** believes that speaking to cars, washing machines, fridges and even our online banks will become the norm.

The report predicts that by 2066, regional accents will become obsolete due to increased social and geographical **(22)**_____, causing a greater   **MOBILE** mingling of accents and colloquialisms. To back up the study, an app, which collects data on the way words are pronounced throughout the UK, has discovered similar results. The aim of the app is to **(23)**_____ map   **ACCURATE** language change in line with the Survey of English Dialects. This survey, which was **(24)**_____   **TAKE** between 1950 and 1961, took thousands of interviews with different classes of people from various parts of the country.

For questions 25–30, complete the second sentence, using the word given, so that it has a similar meaning to the first sentence. Do not change the word provided and use between three and six words in total. In the separate answer sheet, write your answers in capital letters, using one box per letter.

25   Marta was determined to help me pass my driving test.

   INSISTED

   Marta _____ my driving test.

26   According to reports, the driver of the speeding car was a famous athlete.

   BEING

   According to reports, the speeding car _____
   famous athlete.

27   Without James' support, I wouldn't have achieved what I have today.

   BEEN

   If _____ James' support, I don't think I would have
   achieved what I have today.

28   The suspect escaped without punishment due to a strong defence.

   AWAY

   On account of a strong defence, the suspect _____
   punishment.

29   'Did you see the new Tarantino film?' Ahmed asked Jack.

   SEEN

   Ahmed asked Jack _____ the new Tarantino film.

30   My best friend stopped me before I could make a big mistake.

   PREVENTED

   My best friend _____ a big mistake.

Answer sheet: Cambridge C1 Advanced
Use of English

Test No. [ ]

Mark out of 36 [ ]

Name _____ Date _____

Part 1: Multiple choice   8 marks

Mark the appropriate answer (A, B, C or D).

0	A	B	C	D	

1	A	B	C	D			5	A	B	C	D	
2	A	B	C	D			6	A	B	C	D	
3	A	B	C	D			7	A	B	C	D	
4	A	B	C	D			8	A	B	C	D	

Part 2: Open cloze   8 marks

Write your answers in capital letters, using one box per letter.

0	B	E	C	A	U	S	E				

9											
10											
11											
12											
13											
14											
15											
16											

Part 3: Word formation   8 marks

Write your answers in capital letters, using one box per letter.

17

18

19

20

21

22

23

24

Part 4: Key word transformation   12 marks

Write your answers in capital letters, using one box per letter.

25

26

27

28

29

30

Cambridge
C1 Advanced
Use of English

Test 8

For questions 1–8, read the text below and decide which answer best fits each gap. In the separate answer sheet, mark the appropriate answer (A, B, C or D).

Upcycling

Having first appeared in William McDonough's book *Cradle to cradle* in 2002, 'upcycling' means reusing a material without **(1)**_____ its quality and composition for its next use, or, simply put, **(2)**_____ products into new materials of better quality.

Upcycling reduces the amount of waste we produce, as well as the need for new materials to be used when making a product, **(3)**_____ in less energy expended. It is a cyclical process that can **(4)**_____ reduce the amount of waste or rubbish we put into landfill.

Two examples of commonly upcycled products are furniture and clothing. For instance, clothes designers have begun using industrial textile **(5)**_____ and second-hand clothing for their designs. This forms part of the circular economy model, in which products are used for as long as possible, then **(6)**_____ once they are finished with. Furniture also follows this model, with old furniture being restored or **(7)**_____ to form a new **(8)**_____ item.

1	**A** degrading	**B** declining	**C** breaking down	**D** cheapening
2	**A** separating	**B** diverging	**C** varying	**D** transforming
3	**A** finishing	**B** resulting	**C** consequently	**D** arising
4	**A** extremely	**B** drastically	**C** awfully	**D** almost
5	**A** waste	**B** rubbish	**C** mess	**D** sewage
6	**A** repurposed	**B** reallocated	**C** redeployed	**D** reassigned
7	**A** melted down	**B** smashed up	**C** broken down	**D** built up
8	**A** household	**B** home	**C** house	**D** familial

For questions 9–16, read the text below and decide which word best fits each gap. Use only one word for each gap. In the separate answer sheet, write your answers in capital letters, using one box per letter.

Black Panther

Marvel's *Black Panther* became one of the last decade's biggest box office successes, making more than $400 million on **(9)**_____ opening weekend in both the US and overseas.

Not only did it receive rave reviews from critics and a 97% rating on review site Rotten Tomatoes, it quickly became a cultural phenomenon and a revered celebration of black culture. It features an all-star cast of black talent, **(10)**_____ in front of the camera and **(11)**_____ the scenes, and has acted as a career springboard for its main actors, Chadwick Boseman and Michael B Jordan, **(12)**_____ are now two of the most **(13)**_____-demand actors in Hollywood.

Black Panther won numerous awards in various categories, including a BAFTA for Best Special Visual Effects and an Academy Award for Best Costume Design, received by head designer Ruth Carter. Ruth says she was inspired by Kenyan, Namibian and South African colours, materials and textures, which led **(14)**_____ to show tribal diversity in fictional Wakanda, whilst also representing the diversity of black culture itself.

As the first black superhero film in the Marvel™ franchise, and as a superhero film with a larger budget than **(15)**_____ other, *Black Panther* beat all of its expectations and has firmly secured a place as a timeless and groundbreaking film that **(16)**_____ set a precedent for the film industry to follow.

For questions 17–24, use the stem word on the right to form the correct word that fills each gap. In the separate answer sheet, write your answers in capital letters, using one box per letter.

Hip Hop

In the 1970's, New York introduced the world to a new style of music, and its **(17)**_____ continues to influence world culture.   **POPULAR**

Hip Hop began by musicians sampling older tracks over new beats and basslines, and reusing the songs in a new context – known as 'flipping' in Hip Hop culture. The genre is comprised of many elements – from DJing and rapping, to breakdancing and beatboxing. These arts were developed by African-American communities to **(18)**_____ them to make a statement on the   **ABLE** social and **(19)**_____ issues their communities   **POLITICS** faced.

By 1979, Hip Hop music had become a **(20)**_____   **MAIN** genre, and by the 1990's it had begun to influence fashion and culture **(21)**_____.   Nowadays,   it   is   **WORLD** considered 'the world's favourite youth culture', according to *National Geographic*, and almost every country now has its own version of local rap and Hip Hop music.

This year, the Universal Hip Hop Museum is due to open in the Bronx, New York, in **(22)**_____ of the   **CELEBRATE** genre's 50th anniversary. The   museum   is   a **(23)**_____ between Microsoft and a department of   **COLLABORATE** one of the US' most prominent colleges, MIT. The museum will be the first American institution dedicated to all things Hip Hop in the country, and will show the many ways in which Hip Hop has **(23)**_____ affected   **CULTURE** not only local communities, but also the US as a whole.

For questions 25–30, complete the second sentence, using the word given, so that it has a similar meaning to the first sentence. Do not change the word provided and use between three and six words in total. In the separate answer sheet, write your answers in capital letters, using one box per letter.

25   Chris never takes any notice of what his brother says to him.

ATTENTION

Chris never _____ his brother says.

26   The manager postponed the team meeting until later that day.

OFF

The team meeting _____ later than day.

27   Reports say the building was graffitied by local protestors.

ALLEGED

Local protestors _____ graffitied the building.

28   I definitely think Daniella was out late last night, as she looks tired.

MUST

Daniella _____ late last night because she looks tired.

29   'You dropped my phone, didn't you, Jan?' demanded Li.

ACCUSED

Li _____ her phone.

30   I'm really bad at remembering important dates.

MEMORY

I _____ remembering important dates.

Answer sheet: Cambridge C1 Advanced
Use of English

Test No. ☐

Mark out of 36 ☐

Name _____   **Date** _____

Part 1: Multiple choice   8 marks

Mark the appropriate answer (A, B, C or D).

0	A	**B**	C	D

1	A	B	C	D		5	A	B	C	D
2	A	B	C	D		6	A	B	C	D
3	A	B	C	D		7	A	B	C	D
4	A	B	C	D		8	A	B	C	D

Part 2: Open cloze   8 marks

Write your answers in capital letters, using one box per letter.

| 0 | B | E | C | A | U | S | E | | | | |

9										
10										
11										
12										
13										
14										
15										
16										

Part 3: Word formation

8 marks

Write your answers in capital letters, using one box per letter.

17 ⬜⬜⬜⬜⬜⬜⬜⬜⬜⬜⬜

18 ⬜⬜⬜⬜⬜⬜⬜⬜⬜⬜⬜

19 ⬜⬜⬜⬜⬜⬜⬜⬜⬜⬜⬜

20 ⬜⬜⬜⬜⬜⬜⬜⬜⬜⬜⬜

21 ⬜⬜⬜⬜⬜⬜⬜⬜⬜⬜⬜

22 ⬜⬜⬜⬜⬜⬜⬜⬜⬜⬜⬜

23 ⬜⬜⬜⬜⬜⬜⬜⬜⬜⬜⬜

24 ⬜⬜⬜⬜⬜⬜⬜⬜⬜⬜⬜

Part 4: Key word transformation

12 marks

Write your answers in capital letters, using one box per letter.

25 ⬜⬜⬜⬜⬜⬜⬜⬜⬜⬜⬜⬜⬜⬜⬜⬜⬜
⬜⬜⬜⬜⬜⬜⬜⬜⬜⬜⬜⬜⬜⬜⬜⬜⬜

26 ⬜⬜⬜⬜⬜⬜⬜⬜⬜⬜⬜⬜⬜⬜⬜⬜⬜
⬜⬜⬜⬜⬜⬜⬜⬜⬜⬜⬜⬜⬜⬜⬜⬜⬜

27 ⬜⬜⬜⬜⬜⬜⬜⬜⬜⬜⬜⬜⬜⬜⬜⬜⬜
⬜⬜⬜⬜⬜⬜⬜⬜⬜⬜⬜⬜⬜⬜⬜⬜⬜

28 ⬜⬜⬜⬜⬜⬜⬜⬜⬜⬜⬜⬜⬜⬜⬜⬜⬜
⬜⬜⬜⬜⬜⬜⬜⬜⬜⬜⬜⬜⬜⬜⬜⬜⬜

29 ⬜⬜⬜⬜⬜⬜⬜⬜⬜⬜⬜⬜⬜⬜⬜⬜⬜
⬜⬜⬜⬜⬜⬜⬜⬜⬜⬜⬜⬜⬜⬜⬜⬜⬜

30 ⬜⬜⬜⬜⬜⬜⬜⬜⬜⬜⬜⬜⬜⬜⬜⬜⬜
⬜⬜⬜⬜⬜⬜⬜⬜⬜⬜⬜⬜⬜⬜⬜⬜⬜

Cambridge
C1 Advanced
Use of English

Test 9

For questions 1–8, read the text below and decide which answer best fits each gap. In the separate answer sheet, mark the appropriate answer (A, B, C or D).

Searching for Sugar Man

Searching for Sugar Man is an Oscar-winning documentary that tells the story of a Mexican-American songwriter, Sixto Rodriguez, **(1)**_____ first two albums flopped in the early seventies, but ended up being the soundtrack to Apartheid-era South Africa.

Rodriguez had no idea what was happening over the other side of the world, as he carried on with his life in Detroit as a **(2)**_____ musician, working in construction. It was in Australia that his music first became a success, with his track 'Sugar Man' getting radio airplay. Due to a **(3)**_____ of sales in the US, the record company stopped producing the album and copies were **(4)**_____ limited. Little did Rodriguez know that his records would eventually sell for **(5)**_____ of $300.

A South African journalist decided to **(6)**_____ the little-known star down to make a documentary film in the mid-90's, and finally brought him to South Africa to perform three sold-out shows. During Apartheid, international **(7)**_____ imposed on South Africa disallowed communication with the outside world, but Rodriguez's album made its way in and its political lyrics **(8)**_____ with its listeners.

1	A	whose	B	who	C	that	D	which
2	A	failed	B	flopped	C	expelled	D	ousted
3	A	fall	B	decline	C	lack	D	decrease
4	A	such	B	however	C	although	D	therefore
5	A	almost	B	upwards	C	up	D	higher
6	A	track	B	find	C	discover	D	search
7	A	deterrents	B	punishments	C	penalties	D	sanctions
8	A	resonated	B	echoed	C	sounded	D	felt

For questions 9–16, read the text below and decide which word best fits each gap. Use only one word for each gap. In the separate answer sheet, write your answers in capital letters, using one box per letter.

A trip into Space

Virgin Galactic is a commercial spacecraft-development company **(9)**_____ aims to take passengers to space as tourists.

It was founded in 2004 by Richard Branson of the Virgin Group, which also owns the airline Virgin Atlantic. Branson initially predicted that **(10)**_____ maiden voyage to Space would launch in 2009 from its base, Spaceport America, which led to 300 pre-booked ticket sales, priced at $200,000 **(11)**_____. However, after years of delays, Branson finally launched a test flight in 2014 that comprised a new, more powerful rocket engine, the fuel of which was derived from nylon instead of rubber. During the flight, the rocket's air-break device was activated too early, which tragically resulted in a fatal crash.

(12)_____ events have done nothing to deter the company, which now has more than 600 customers **(13)**_____ 60 countries signed **(14)**_____ for the 90-minute flight. It aims to escape the Earth's atmosphere to see the planet's curviture from Space and allow passengers to experience weightlessness. However, Virgin Galactic faces tough competition from SpaceX, owned by Tesla entrepreneur Elon Musk, which is planning a passenger flight around the Moon in 2023.

(15)_____ 2018, Virgin Galactic has successfully reached suborbital Space more than once, earning five pilots **(16)**_____ commercial astronaut wings. Owner Richard Branson has said he will go up in a test flight himself later this year.

For questions 17–24, use the stem word on the right to form the correct word that fills each gap. In the separate answer sheet, write your answers in capital letters, using one box per letter.

Margaret Atwood

As Canada's most eminent novelist, Margaret Atwood has written over 20 published titles, translated into 30 languages. She is best known for her prose fiction and for writing from a **(17)**_____ perspective.   **FEMININE**

Born in 1939, Atwood spent most of her **(18)**_____ living in the forests of northern Canada   **CHILD** with her parents. She began writing aged just five, and went on to achieve a master's degree in English **(19)**_____ in 1962.   **LITERATE**

Her first **(20)**_____ was a book of poetry in 1961   **PUBLISH** that celebrated the natural world and condemned **(21)**_____, a theme often prevalent in her books   **MATERIAL** to this day. She then ventured into writing novels whilst working as an English teacher, becoming a full-time writer in 1972.

Since then, she has held a variety of **(22)**_____   **PRESTIGE** posts, such as president of numerous literary societies, and has won multiple awards, including the 2019 and 2020 Booker Prizes and the Arthur C. Clark award for Best Science-fiction Novel.

Recently, her stories have gained a new wave of readers, particularly of her 1985 book *The Handmaid's Tale*, which, in 2017, was adapted for a TV series that went on to win multiple Emmy Awards, including Outstanding Drama Series. This has led to talk of other possible **(23)**_____ of Margaret's books, including *The*   **ADAPT** *Testaments*, the **(24)**_____ released and highly   **NEW** anticipated follow-up to *The Handmaid's Tale*.

Part 4   Key word transformation   Test 9

For questions 25–30, complete the second sentence, using the word given, so that it has a similar meaning to the first sentence. Do not change the word provided and use between three and six words in total. In the separate answer sheet, write your answers in capital letters, using one box per letter.

25 I expect I'll move out of my parents' house before I'm 25.

   TIME

   By _____ 25, I expect I'll have moved out of my parents' house.

26 I'd planned to meet up with an old friend this weekend, but she let me down.

   GOING

   I _____ with an old school friend this weekend, but she cancelled.

27 I wanted to visit Luca at the weekend, but I heard he'd gone to Italy to see his family.

   WOULD

   I _____ Luca at the weekend, but I heard he'd gone to Italy to see his family.

28 The only thing I didn't love about the wedding was the music at the reception.

   FROM

   I loved everything about the wedding _____ at the reception.

29 'I think you should seriously consider getting a new job if they treat you that badly,' my friend said.

   SUGGESTED

   My friend _____ getting a new job.

30 Many people have been saying that we depend too much on technology nowadays.

   ARGUED

   It _____ we depend too much on technology nowadays.

Answer sheet: Cambridge C1 Advanced
Use of English

Test No. ☐

Mark out of 36 ☐

Name _____   **Date** _____

Part 1: Multiple choice   8 marks

Mark the appropriate answer (A, B, C or D).

0	A	**B**	C	D	

1	A	B	C	D			5	A	B	C	D	
2	A	B	C	D			6	A	B	C	D	
3	A	B	C	D			7	A	B	C	D	
4	A	B	C	D			8	A	B	C	D	

Part 2: Open cloze   8 marks

Write your answers in capital letters, using one box per letter.

0	B	E	C	A	U	S	E				

9										
10										
11										
12										
13										
14										
15										
16										

Part 3: Word formation   8 marks

Write your answers in capital letters, using one box per letter.

17										

18										

19										

20										

21										

22										

23										

24										

Part 4: Key word transformation   12 marks

Write your answers in capital letters, using one box per letter.

25															

26															

27															

28															

29															

30															

Cambridge C1 Advanced Use of English

Test 10

For questions 1–8, read the text below and decide which answer best fits each gap. In the separate answer sheet, mark the appropriate answer (A, B, C or D).

Sony Playstation

In December 1994, the original Playstation was **(1)**_____ in Japan. It went on to become the first-ever video game to sell more than 100 million units, and is one of the most popular game **(2)**_____ to this day.

The Playstation 1 was slimmer and easier to control than its **(3)**_____ and was released much earlier into international markets than its competitors, allowing it to **(4)**_____ the larger market share. In 1995, it was released on pre-sale at the Electronic Entertainment Expo in Los Angeles and had already sold 100,000 **(5)**_____ before its launch four months later.

(6)_____ then, there have been four new Playstation releases, with the Playstation 2 (PS2) being the best-selling console to date. This was due largely to its memory size, and its **(7)**_____ with PS1 games, which was a rare feature at the time. However, the latest iteration, the PS4, takes the **(8)**_____ of fastest-selling console, with more than one million units sold in its first day on the market.

1	A	opened	B	launched	C	initiated	D	born
2	A	consoles	B	equipment	C	instruments	D	devices
3	A	equivalents	B	allies	C	contestants	D	competitors
4	A	win	B	earn	C	prize	D	set
5	A	units	B	things	C	objects	D	items
6	A	For	B	Since	C	Until	D	From
7	A	useage	B	agreement	C	similarity	D	compatibility
8	A	title	B	headline	C	name	D	header

For questions 9–16, read the text below and decide which word best fits each gap. Use only one word for each gap. In the separate answer sheet, write your answers in capital letters, using one box per letter.

High-heeled shoes

The first recorded instance of a high-heeled shoe being worn was in the 16th century by Catherine de Medici, who stood **(9)**_____ only around 150 centimetres tall. It is said she chose to wear the unorthodox footwear to look taller at her wedding, regardless of the shock it may have caused amongst the guests. Prior to this, believe it or not, high-heeled shoes had only been seen on men.

(10)_____ remained the case long after de Medici died, as, for around 200 years, men were still the only gender to wear such shoes. This was to allow them to look tall and powerful, **(11)**_____ women opted for lower heels or small platforms to represent **(12)**_____ place in society at the time. Louis XIV of France became famous for his statement 'red heel', while other members of the French court wore yellow, silk shoes with a 'Louis' heel, later named **(13)**_____ the King.

Following the end of World War II, there was a shift, as men continued to wear the flat shoes and boots they had used in the war effort. In the 1950's, the stiletto heel was born, which made heels **(14)**_____ they are today. The movement began by women wearing stiletto heels in prominent advertisements for beauty products, which paved **(15)**_____ way for more ladies to begin wearing them as their day-to-day shoe.

However, in recent years, some researchers have argued that high heels can cause long-lasting damage to both the feet and back, as well as pressure to one's blood circulation, **(16)**_____ can lead to swelling and varicose veins.

For questions 17–24, use the stem word on the right to form the correct word that fills each gap. In the separate answer sheet, write your answers in capital letters, using one box per letter.

Bonsai trees

Originating in the Chinese Empire, Bonsai is an art-form combining horticultural techniques and Asian aesthetics. Bonsai trees are small trees that mimic the shape and style of a fully-grown tree.

Bonsai trees need to be cared for **(17)**_____, by feeding, watering, pruning and eventually repotting. Each species of Bonsai requires a different method of care, including a variety of light conditions and climates.
DAY

Over centuries, the art of Japanese Bonsai has established traditions, techniques and design guidelines. 'Bon–sai', **(18)**_____ translated as 'planted in a container', means that the trees always need to be kept potted, and a percentage of the leaves need to be cut off to ensure the Bonsai tree **(19)**_____ its roots. A wire is used to direct the **(20)**_____ of the branches, and the tree must be kept small yet have a mature **(21)**_____. The ultimate goal of Bonsai is to create a **(22)**_____ depiction of nature.
LITERAL

GENERATE
GROW

APPEAR
REAL

There are several **(23)**_____ of Bonsai tree, depending on their size, the smallest measuring 3–8 cm in height and the largest standing at 152–203 cm tall. The **(24)**_____ of a Bonsai tree, with the right care applied, often through generations of owners, can be anywhere from decades to thousands of years.
CLASS

LIFE

For questions 25–30, complete the second sentence, using the word given, so that it has a similar meaning to the first sentence. Do not change the word provided and use between three and six words in total. In the separate answer sheet, write your answers in capital letters, using one box per letter.

25   My teacher doesn't tolerate students being late for class – he won't let them enter the classroom.

   UP

   My teacher _____ being late for class – he won't let them enter the classroom.

26   What the astronomer discovered was something never seen before.

   MADE

   The _____ something never seen before.

27   The birth rate in the country had fallen dramatically over the last few years.

   STEEP

   There _____ in the number of births in the country over the last few years.

28   'I'm sorry I took your car out without permission,' Akira said.

   APOLOGISED

   Akira _____ the car without permission.

29   I knew I had to be there on time for when the surprise happened.

   NECESSARY

   I knew _____ me to be there for when the surprise happened.

30   The ferry's time of departure can change depending on the weather.

   SUBJECT

   The departure time of the ferry _____ the weather.

Answer sheet: Cambridge C1 Advanced
Use of English

Test No. ☐

Mark out of 36 ☐

Name _____ **Date** _____

Part 1: Multiple choice   **8 marks**

Mark the appropriate answer (A, B, C or D).

0	A	**B**	C	D

1	A	B	C	D		5	A	B	C	D
2	A	B	C	D		6	A	B	C	D
3	A	B	C	D		7	A	B	C	D
4	A	B	C	D		8	A	B	C	D

Part 2: Open cloze   **8 marks**

Write your answers in capital letters, using one box per letter.

0	B	E	C	A	U	S	E			

9										
10										
11										
12										
13										
14										
15										
16										

Part 3: Word formation

8 marks

Write your answers in capital letters, using one box per letter.

17

18

19

20

21

22

23

24

Part 4: Key word transformation

12 marks

Write your answers in capital letters, using one box per letter.

25

26

27

28

29

30

Answers

Part 1: Multiple choice

1	A	ranked	5	B	widely
2	C	displaced	6	B	almost
3	D	despite	7	D	afield
4	A	pursue	8	C	spread out

Part 2: Open cloze

9	as	13	in
10	on	14	have
11	which / that	15	when
12	each	16	been

Part 3: Word formation

17	increasingly	21	worrying
18	permission / permits	22	unmistakable
19	enthusiasts	23	significance
20	reuse	24	awareness

Part 4: Key word transformation

25	under no obligation	to
26	not nearly	as big as / as large as
27	will be put down	to
28	not been for	your help
29	can't have	seen Max
30	prevent him from	interfering

Part 1: Multiple choice						
1	**D**	ritual	**5**	**A**	cleansed
2	**B**	hospitality	**6**	**D**	honour
3	**A**	atmosphere	**7**	**A**	gain
4	**B**	equipment	**8**	**B**	revered

Part 2: Open cloze			
9	in	**13**	less
10	or	**14**	some
11	by	**15**	number
12	this / so	**16**	such

Part 3: Word formation			
17	pollinate	**21**	implications
18	fertilising	**22**	populations
19	threatened	**23**	temperatures
20	greatly	**24**	unlikely

Part 4: Key word transformation		
25	takes me	for granted
26	the chances were	of
27	was	considerably better
28	not how	a sensible person
29	carried out / had carried out	the task
30	it hadn't / it had not been	for

Part 1: Multiple choice

1	A	border	5	B	dip
2	B	within	6	C	existence
3	D	heavily	7	D	erosion
4	c	although	8	C	away

Part 2: Open cloze

9	back	13	However
10	one	14	Another
11	not	15	to
12	Of	16	Despite

Part 3: Word formation

17	popularity	21	accompaniment
18	objective	22	enthusiastically
19	inflatable / inflated	23	uniquely
20	oversees	24	coordination

Part 4: Key word transformation

25	is being	pulled down
26	wasn't in the mood	for
27	If only	I was / I were
28	on good terms	with
29	come up with	a solution
30	were (only) slightly	better

Part 1: Multiple choice

1	B	Developed	5	B	against
2	A	which	6	D	worth
3	A	stiff	7	C	yet
4	C	such	8	A	transformed

Part 2: Open cloze

9	being	13	no
10	which	14	as
11	been	15	will
12	since	16	made

Part 3: Word formation

17	generation	21	publicly
18	sought	22	accurately
19	replace	23	container
20	following	24	acceptance

Part 4: Key word transformation

25	the more nervous	I get
26	before had I	seen
27	I'd rather / I would rather	go to
28	looks down	on
29	be	of (any) assistance
30	signed up to / signed up for	Russian

Part 1: Multiple choice

1	C	by	5	A	variety
2	D	persona	6	C	took
3	B	gig	7	D	contestant
4	B	audience	8	C	undoubtedly

Part 2: Open cloze

9	come	13	it
10	by	14	what
11	had	15	these
12	were	16	who / that

Part 3: Word formation

17	historical	21	latest
18	mysteriously	22	impressive
19	unknown	23	immersive
20	constantly	24	renewed

Part 4: Key word transformation

25	make up	a story to
26	told her	without hesitation
27	make you	cool down / cooler / feel cooler
28	I would buy / I'd buy	the tickets / tickets
29	is claimed (that)	scientists / the scientists
30	as long as	the weather

Part 1: Multiple choice

1	A	trend	5	B	boost
2	C	Originating	6	C	hint
3	A	properties	7	D	region
4	D	treat	8	B	cultivation

Part 2: Open cloze

9	it	13	in
10	must	14	had
11	so	15	off
12	by	16	all

Part 3: Word formation

17	ethnicity	21	originally
18	scholarship	22	political
19	marriage	23	organiser
20	relocated	24	collective

Part 4: Key word transformation

25	make the most	of being / staying
26	let	the team down / let down the team
27	has been an increase	in
28	If only	I had gone
29	hesitate to call	me if
30	ought to have	told/informed me (that) / let me know (that)

Part 1: Multiple choice

1	C	founded	5	C	interest
2	B	people	6	B	rose
3	B	Collectively	7	A	eventually
4	A	publish	8	D	fund

Part 2: Open cloze

9	was	13	until
10	been	14	its/the
11	where	15	their
12	whose	16	in

Part 3: Word formation

17	significantly	21	findings
18	shortened	22	mobility
19	entirely	23	accurately
20	interactions	24	undertaken

Part 4: Key word transformation

25	insisted on helping	me pass
26	was being driven	by a
27	it hadn't / it had not been	for
28	got away	without (any)
29	if	he had seen
30	prevented me from	making

Part 1: Multiple choice

1	A	degrading	5	A	waste
2	D	transforming	6	A	repurposed
3	B	resulting	7	C	broken down
4	B	drastically	8	A	household

Part 2: Open cloze

9	its	13	in
10	both	14	her
11	behind	15	any
12	who	16	has

Part 3: Word formation

17	popularity	21	worldwide
18	enable	22	celebration
19	political	23	collaboration
20	mainstream	24	culturally

Part 4: Key word transformation

25	pays attention	to what
26	was put off	until
27	are	alleged to have
28	must have	been out
29	accused Jan of	dropping / cracking / breaking
30	have a (really) bad memory	for

Part 1: Multiple choice

1	A	whose	5	B	upwards
2	A	failed	6	A	track
3	C	lack	7	D	sanctions
4	D	therefore	8	A	resonated

Part 2: Open cloze

9	that / which	13	from
10	the	14	up
11	each	15	Since
12	These	16	their

Part 3: Word formation

17	feminist	21	materialism
18	childhood	22	prestigious
19	literature	23	adaptations
20	publication	24	newly

Part 4: Key word transformation

25	the time	I'm / I am
26	was going to	meet up
27	would	have visited
28	apart from	the music
29	suggested (that) I should	seriously consider
30	has been argued	that

Part 1: Multiple choice

1	B	launched	5	A	units
2	A	consoles	6	B	Since
3	D	competitors	7	D	compatibility
4	A	win	8	A	title

Part 2: Open cloze

9	at	13	after
10	This	14	what
11	while	15	the
12	their	16	which

Part 3: Word formation

17	daily	21	appearance
18	literally	22	realistic
19	regenerates	23	classifications
20	growth	24	lifespan

Part 4: Key word transformation

25	doesn't / does not put up with	students
26	discovery (that/which) the astronomer made / astronomer made a discovery which/that	was
27	had been a steep	fall/decline
28	apologised for	taking (out) / using / driving
29	it was necessary	for
30	is subject	to

Notes

Notes

Notes